PRAYING
GOD'S WILL
for
My Grandchild

LEE ROBERTS

OLIVER
NELSON

THOMAS NELSON PUBLISHERS
Nashville • Atlanta • London • Vancouver

This book is dedicated to
Kaitlynn Nicole Howe,
my first grandchild.

Copyright © 1995 by Lee Roberts

Published in Nashville, Tennessee, by Thomas Nelson, Inc., Publishers, and distributed in Canada by Word Communications, Ltd., Richmond, British Columbia.

The Bible version used in this publication is THE NEW KING JAMES VERSION. Copyright © 1979, 1980, 1982, Thomas Nelson, Inc., Publishers. Verses have been modified to fit the prayer format.

Library of Congress Cataloging-in-Publication Data

Roberts, Lee, 1941–
    Praying God's will for my grandchild / Lee Roberts.
        p. cm.
    ISBN 0-7852-7919-9 (pbk.)
    1. Grandparents—Prayer-books and devotions—English. 2. Grandparent and child. I. Title.
BV4528.5.R63   1995
242'.845—dc20   94-34819
                                                                            CIP

Printed in the United States of America.

1 2 3 4 5 6 — 99 98 97 96 95

Contents

For Grandparents Only

To be the grandchild of a Christian grandparent is a wonderful privilege for the grandchild and an awesome responsibility for the grandparent. Since this is a book for you, the grandparents, the first and foremost consideration is to invoke the blessings of God in all areas of your grandchild's life. That includes not only his spiritual life but also his emotional, intellectual, and physical lives. And you will want to pray for her on a daily basis.

Fortunately, God has given you the perfect prayers for all areas of your grandchild's life. Those prayers are found in the Bible, the Word of God. Matthew 4:4 and Ephesians 6:17 provide abundant instructions to pray God's Word directly from Scripture and to do it consistently.

Be encouraged by the fact that by praying God's Word you are actually praying God's mind and perfect will for your grandchild. But perhaps the greatest encouragement of all will be that you will see each grandchild grow in his or her love for God and His blessings on them.

All chapters deal with concerns for both grand-daughters and grandsons. But to deal with the pro-noun problems, odd-numbered chapters use the masculine pronoun and even-numbered chapters use the feminine pronoun.

1
ANGER

Heavenly Father, I thank You for all that You do for my grandchild. In Jesus' name, I humbly ask You today to hear and honor my prayers concerning any anger that may abide in my grandchild. Your words are clear that anger will not produce the righteousness that You want in him. At this very moment I ask You to remove any and all anger from this child that I love so much. Thank You, God, for answering my prayers.

**God, in accordance
with Your word . . .**

I pray that my grandchild will be swift to hear, slow to speak, slow to wrath; for his wrath does not produce the righteousness of God.

JAMES 1:19–20

I pray that the discretion of my grandchild makes him slow to anger, and it is to his glory to over-look a transgression.

PROVERBS 19:11

I pray that my grandchild will not hasten in his spirit to be angry, for anger rests in the bosom of fools.

ECCLESIASTES 7:9

I pray that my grandchild will commit his way to You, LORD, and trust also in You, and You shall bring it to pass. You shall bring forth his righteous-ness as the light, and his justice as the noonday. I pray that he will rest in You, LORD, and wait pa-tiently for You. I pray that he does not fret be-cause of him who prospers in his way or because of the man who brings wicked schemes to pass. I pray that he will cease from anger, and forsake wrath; that he does not fret—it only causes harm.

PSALM 37:5–8

I pray that my grandchild will let all bitterness, wrath, anger, clamor, and evil speaking be put away from him, with all malice. I pray also that he will be kind to others, tenderhearted, forgiving others, just as God in Christ also forgave him.

EPHESIANS 4:31–32

❀

I pray that my grandchild understands that a fool vents all his feelings, but a wise person holds his back.

PROVERBS 29:11

❀

I pray that my grandchild knows that being slow to anger is better than the mighty and ruling his spirit is better than taking a city.

PROVERBS 16:32

❀

I pray that my grandchild realizes that a person who is quick-tempered acts foolishly.

PROVERBS 14:17

Brandon
Kendall
Tierney
Jaclyan
Cameron
Sidney
Chase
Ashlynn
Taylor
Lauren Angel with God
Brooke
Reagan
Devynn
Austin

2
ATTITUDE

Lord Jesus, I ask You now, using the very words that have been given to me in the holy Scriptures, to make certain that my grandchild always has an attitude of joy in You and an attitude and an expectancy that she can do all things through You who give her Your strength to face the issues and problems of life. Thank You, Lord, for her happiness and her joy. In Your name I pray. Amen.

**God, in accordance
with Your word . . .**

I pray that my grandchild knows that she can do all things through Christ who strengthens her.

PHILIPPIANS 4:13

I pray that my grandchild will not sorrow, for the joy of the LORD is her strength.

NEHEMIAH 8:10

I pray that my grandchild will remember whatever things are true, whatever things are noble, whatever things are just, whatever things are pure, whatever things are lovely, whatever things are of good report, if there is any virtue and if there is anything praiseworthy—that she will meditate on these things.

PHILIPPIANS 4:8

I pray that my grandchild will remember that this is the day the LORD has made and that she will rejoice and be glad in it.

PSALM 118:24

I pray that my grandchild understands what Jesus meant when He said, "My grace is sufficient for you, for My strength is made perfect in weakness."

2 CORINTHIANS 12:9

I pray that my grandchild realizes that in all these things she is more than a conqueror through You who loved her.

ROMANS 8:37

I pray that my grandchild will always love You, the Lord her God, with all her heart, with all her soul, with all her mind, and with all her strength and that she will love her neighbor as herself.

MARK 12:30–31

I pray that whatever my grandchild does she does it heartily, as to You, Lord, and not to men.

COLOSSIANS 3:23

Kendall

Tierney

Jaclynn

Sidney

Taylor

Lauren Angel w/ Dad

Brooke

Ashylynn

Devlynn Lea

3

CONDEMNED

Lord God, I ask You to keep in my grandchild's mind at all times that there is no condemnation for those that are in Christ Jesus. Help him to know that if he trusts in Jesus he need not let Satan bring thoughts of doubt and condemnation in his mind. Thank You, Lord, for removing all such thoughts and feelings from my grandchild. In Jesus' name. Amen.

**God, in accordance
with Your word . . .**

I pray that my grandchild will draw near with a true heart in full assurance of faith, having his heart sprinkled from an evil conscience and his body washed with pure water.

HEBREWS 10:22

———— ✳ ————

I pray that my grandchild always remembers that You, the LORD his God, are gracious and merciful,

and will not turn Your face from him if he returns
to You.

2 CHRONICLES 30:9

I pray that my grandchild knows that it was You,
God, who said that, "I, even I, am He who blots
out your transgressions for My own sake."

ISAIAH 43:25

I pray, God, that You did not send Your Son into
the world to condemn my grandchild, but that my
grandchild through Him might be saved. He who
believes in Him is not condemned.

JOHN 3:17–18

I pray that my grandchild, who hears Your word,
Jesus, and believes in Him who sent You has everlasting life, and shall not come into judgment, but
has passed from death into life.

JOHN 5:24

I pray that You, God, will be merciful to my grand-child's unrighteousness, and to his sins, and to his lawless deeds and that You remember them no more.

HEBREWS 8:12

I pray that my grandchild will forsake any wicked ways and any unrighteous thoughts. Let him re-turn to You, LORD, and You will have mercy on him and abundantly pardon him.

ISAIAH 55:7

I pray that my grandchild will acknowledge his sin to You, God, and his iniquity he has not hid-den. That he will confess his transgressions to You so You can forgive the iniquity of his sins.

PSALM 32:5

4
CONFIDENCE

Lord Jesus, based upon God's words I call upon You to literally fill my grandchild with confidence. Give her the spiritual confidence to know that whatever she asks in Your name she will receive. Fill her with the confidence that only You can give. Thank You for honoring Your words and my prayers. Amen.

**God, in accordance
with Your word . . .**

I pray that when my grandchild passes through the waters, You will be with her; and through the rivers, they shall not overflow her. When she walks through the fire, she shall not be burned, nor shall the flame scorch her.

ISAIAH 43:2

I pray, God, that my grandchild always remembers that it is You who justifies.

ROMANS 8:33

───────── ❋ ─────────

I pray that this is the confidence that my grandchild has in You, Jesus, that if she asks anything according to Your will, You hear her. And if she knows that You hear her, whatever she asks, she knows that she has the petitions that she asked of You.

1 JOHN 5:14–15

───────── ❋ ─────────

I pray that when my grandchild faces an obstacle she always remembers that God has said that it is "Not by might nor by power, but by My Spirit."

ZECHARIAH 4:6

───────── ❋ ─────────

I pray that whatever my grandchild asks in Jesus' name, You will do it.

JOHN 14:14

I pray that You, the LORD God, are my grand-child's strength.

HABAKKUK 3:19

------------- ❋ -------------

I pray that my grandchild will not cast away her confidence, which has great reward. For she has need of endurance, so that after she has done the will of You, God, she may receive the promise.

HEBREWS 10:35–36

------------- ❋ -------------

I pray that my grandchild will be confident of this very thing, that You who have begun a good work in her will complete it until the day of Jesus Christ.

PHILIPPIANS 1:6

------------- ❋ -------------

I pray that my grandchild can do all things through Christ who strengthens her.

PHILIPPIANS 4:13

5
CONFUSED

Heavenly Father, in the beautiful and precious name of Jesus, my Lord and my Savior, I ask You to remove all confusion from my grandchild. Help him to know that You are the author of peace and not of confusion and that he is to lean on You and Your words and not his own understanding. Thank You for honoring this prayer for my wonderful and precious grandchild. Amen.

**God, in accordance
with Your word ...**

I pray that my grandchild will trust in You, LORD, with all his heart, and lean not on his own understanding. I pray that in all his ways he will acknowledge You, and You will direct his paths.

PROVERBS 3:5–6

I pray that You, God, will instruct my grandchild and teach him in the way he should go.

PSALM 32:8

———— ✾ ————

I pray that my grandchild has great peace because he loves Your law, and nothing can cause him to stumble.

PSALM 119:165

———— ✾ ————

I pray that my grandchild will always cast his burdens on You, LORD, and You shall sustain him.

PSALM 55:22

———— ✾ ————

I pray that my grandchild will be anxious for nothing, but in everything by prayer and supplication, with thanksgiving, let his requests be made known to You, God, and the peace of God, which surpasses all understanding, will guard his heart and mind through Christ Jesus.

PHILIPPIANS 4:6–7

I pray that my grandchild will always remember that God gives power to the weak, and to those who have no might He increases strength.

ISAIAH 40:29

I pray that when my grandchild feels confused he will remember and understand that You, God, are not the author of confusion but of peace.

1 CORINTHIANS 14:33

I pray that my grandchild knows that where envy and self-seeking exist, confusion and every evil thing will be there. But the wisdom that is from above is first pure, then peaceable, gentle, willing to yield, full of mercy and good fruits, without partiality and without hypocrisy.

JAMES 3:16–17

6
COURAGE

Perfect God, grant my grandchild the courage that only You can give. Help her to remember that she can do all things through Jesus and that she should never be afraid or discouraged or dismayed because You, her God, will be with her always. Thank You, God, in Jesus' name, for filling my grandchild with courage. Amen.

**God, in accordance
with Your word . . .**

I pray that my grandchild will always fear not, for You, God, are with her. I pray that she will not be dismayed, for You are her God. I pray that You will strengthen her and help her and that You will uphold her with Your righteous right hand.

ISAIAH 41:10

I pray that my grandchild will be persuaded that neither death nor life, nor angels nor principalities nor powers, nor things present nor things to come, nor height nor depth, nor any other created thing, shall be able to separate her from the love of God which is in Christ Jesus, her Lord.

ROMANS 8:38–39

I pray that my grandchild shall not die, but live, and declare the works of the LORD.

PSALM 118:17

I pray that You, the eternal God, are my grandchild's refuge and that You will thrust out the enemy from before her.

DEUTERONOMY 33:27

I pray that my grandchild can do all things through Christ who strengthens her.

PHILIPPIANS 4:13

I pray that my grandchild will wait on You, LORD; that she will be of good courage, and You shall strengthen her heart.

PSALM 27:14

I pray that my grandchild does not think it strange concerning the fiery trial which is to try her, as though some strange thing happened to her; but that she will rejoice to the extent that she partakes of Christ's sufferings, that when His glory is revealed, she may also be glad with exceeding joy.

1 PETER 4:12–13

I pray that while my grandchild's weeping may endure for a night, joy comes to her in the morning.

PSALM 30:5

I pray that my grandchild will be of good courage and that You shall strengthen her heart, for her hope is in You, LORD.

PSALM 31:24

7
DELIVERANCE

Lord Jesus, today, at this very moment, I ask You to deliver my grandchild from anything that is adversely afflicting him in any way. Help him to know the truth that comes only from You and Your words and to be set free from all that is upon him. Thank You, Jesus, for freeing my grandchild and for filling him with joy and hope. Amen.

**God, in accordance
with Your word . . .**

I pray that my grandchild shall know the truth,
and the truth shall make him free.

JOHN 8:32

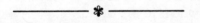

I pray that if You, Jesus, make my grandchild free,
he shall be free indeed.

JOHN 8:36

I pray that there is therefore now no condemnation to my grandchild who is in Christ Jesus, who does not walk according to the flesh, but according to the Spirit. For the law of the Spirit of life in Christ Jesus has made him free from the law of sin and death.

ROMANS 8:1–2

I pray that my grandchild does not believe every spirit, but that he tests the spirits, whether they are of You, God; because many false prophets have gone out into the world. I pray that by this he will know the Spirit of God: that every spirit that confesses that Jesus Christ has come in the flesh is of God.

1 JOHN 4:1–2

I pray that He who is in my grandchild is greater than he who is in the world.

1 JOHN 4:4

8
DEPRESSED

Lord God, I pray to You now as always in Jesus' name. I ask You to remove any depression that may come upon my grandchild at any time. Help her to know, if she will cry out to You, You will hear and deliver her. I ask You to honor Your words and to deliver her from any depression that she may ever experience. In Jesus' name. Amen.

God, in accordance with Your word . . .

I pray that my righteous grandchild will cry out, and You will hear and deliver her out of all of her troubles.

PSALM 34:17

❈

I pray, God, that You are the God of my grandchild's strength.

PSALM 43:2

I pray that while my grandchild's weeping may endure for a night, her joy comes in the morning.

PSALM 30:5

I pray that my grandchild will wait on You, LORD. That she shall renew her strength. That she shall mount up with wings like eagles; that she shall run and not be weary and that she shall walk and not faint.

ISAIAH 40:31

I pray, God, that You will comfort my grandchild in all her tribulation, that she may be able to comfort those who are in any trouble, with the comfort with which she herself is comforted by You.

2 CORINTHIANS 1:4

I pray that my grandchild does not think it strange concerning the fiery trial which is to try her, as though some strange thing has happened to her; but that she will rejoice to the extent that she partakes of Christ's sufferings, so that when His glory is revealed, she may also be glad with exceeding joy.

1 PETER 4:12–13

I pray that whatever things are true, whatever things are noble, whatever things are just, whatever things are pure, whatever things are lovely, whatever things are of good report, if there is any virtue and if there is anything praiseworthy—that my grandchild will meditate on these things.

PHILIPPIANS 4:8

I pray, God, that You will heal my grandchild's broken heart and bind up her wounds.

PSALM 147:3

9
DESERTED BY LOVED ONES

Heavenly Father, I plead with You at this moment to honor Your words and to set my grandchild on high. Your word has promised that You will never leave him or forsake him, no matter what his loved ones might do. He needs You now. Draw him close to You and carry his burdens for him. In the name of Your Son, Jesus, I pray. Amen.

God, in accordance with Your word . . .

I pray that because You have set Your love upon my grandchild, therefore You will deliver him; You will set him on high, because he has known Your name. I pray that he shall call upon You, and You will answer him; You will be with him in trouble; You will deliver him and honor him. That with long life You will satisfy him, and show him Your salvation.

PSALM 91:14–16

I pray, God, that You will not forsake my grandchild nor destroy him.

DEUTERONOMY 4:31

I pray that my grandchild will cast all his cares upon You, God, for You care for him.

1 PETER 5:7

I pray that while my grandchild is hard pressed on every side, yet he is not crushed; he is perplexed, but not in despair; persecuted, but not forsaken; struck down, but not destroyed—always carrying about in his body the dying of the Lord Jesus, that the life of Jesus also may be manifested in his body.

2 CORINTHIANS 4:8–10

I pray that my grandchild will no longer be termed forsaken and You will delight in him.

ISAIAH 62:4

I pray that because my grandchild knows Your name, God, he will put his trust in You; for You, LORD, have not forsaken those who seek You.

PSALM 9:10

---- ❀ ----

I pray that if my grandchild's father and mother forsake him that You will take care of him.

PSALM 27:10

---- ❀ ----

I pray that my grandchild will be taught to observe all things that Jesus has commanded and that he knows that You are with him always, even to the end of the age.

MATTHEW 28:20

---- ❀ ----

I pray that my grandchild always remembers that You will not forget him.

ISAIAH 49:15

10
DISCOURAGED

Perfect God, in Jesus' name I ask You to remove from my grandchild any discouragement that she may be feeling at this time in her life. Teach her what Your words mean when You say to wait on You, and to be of good courage and that You, God, will strengthen her. Thank You for hearing and honoring Your words. Amen.

**God, in accordance
with Your word . . .**

I pray that my grandchild will wait on You, LORD; that she will be of good courage, and that You will strengthen her heart.

PSALM 27:14

I pray that my grandchild shall obtain joy and gladness and that sorrow and sighing shall flee away.

ISAIAH 51:11

I pray that my grandchild will not cast away her confidence, which has great reward. For she has need of endurance, so that after she has done Your will, God, she may receive her promise.

HEBREWS 10:35–36

I pray that my grandchild is confident of this very thing, that You, God, who have begun a good work in her will complete it until the day of Jesus Christ.

PHILIPPIANS 1:6

I pray that my grandchild does not grow weary while doing good, for in due season she shall reap if she does not lose heart.

GALATIANS 6:9

I pray that my grandchild will greatly rejoice, though now for a little while, if need be, she may be grieved by various trials. I pray that the genuineness of her faith, being much more precious than gold that perishes, though it is tested by fire, may be found to praise, honor, and glory at the revelation of Jesus Christ, whom having not seen, she loves. Though now she does not see Him, yet believing, she rejoices with joy inexpressible and full of glory, receiving the end of her faith—the salvation of her soul.

1 PETER 1:6–9

I pray that in everything my grandchild will be anxious for nothing, but in everything by prayer and supplication, with thanksgiving, lets her request be made known to You, God; and Your peace, which surpasses all understanding, will guard her heart and mind through Christ Jesus.

PHILIPPIANS 4:6–7

11
DISSATISFIED

Lord Jesus, through the power of Your perfect and error-free words, I call upon You to replace any dissatisfaction in my grandchild's life with joy, hope, and happiness. Your words say his soul will be satisfied, and he shall have every good thing. Through my faith and the authority of Your word, I now pray Your words for my grandchild and ask that You hear and honor these words from the Bible. Thank You for hearing my prayers. Amen.

**God, in accordance
with Your word . . .**

I pray that my grandchild can do all things through Christ who strengthens him.

PHILIPPIANS 4:13

I pray that my grandchild's soul shall be satisfied as with marrow and fatness, and his mouth shall praise You with joyful lips.

PSALM 63:5

I pray that my grandchild will be satisfied with good by the fruit of his mouth.

PROVERBS 12:14

I pray that because my grandchild seeks You, LORD, he shall not lack any good thing.

PSALM 34:10

I pray that my grandchild will delight himself in You, LORD, and You shall give him the desires of his heart.

PSALM 37:4

I pray that my grandchild will bless You, LORD, with all that is within him and that he will forget

not all Your benefits. I pray that he will not forget
who forgives all his iniquities and who heals all
his diseases. I pray that he will not forget who re-
deems his life from destruction and who crowns
him with lovingkindness and tender mercies and
who satisfies his mouth with good things, so that
his youth is renewed like the eagle's.

PSALM 103:1–5

I pray, God, that You will satisfy my grandchild's
longing soul, and fill his hungry soul with goodness.

PSALM 107:9

I pray that my grandchild will trust and not be
afraid; for You, God, are his strength and his song.
You have become his salvation.

ISAIAH 12:2

12
DISTRESS/SADNESS

God in heaven, You have promised the comfort of the Holy Spirit to us in times such as this. I ask You for a special comforting for my grandchild. Your words say, while sadness may come upon her, her joy will return in the morning. I pray this, Your words, for my grandchild. Remove her distress. Take her sadness. And honor these Your words that I am about to pray. Thank You in Jesus' name. Amen.

**God, in accordance
with Your word . . .**

I pray that my grandchild has done justice and righteousness and that You will not leave her to her oppressors.

PSALM 119:121

I pray that while my grandchild may be despised, she does not forget Your precepts.

PSALM 119:141

I pray that while trouble and anguish have overtaken my grandchild, Your commandments are her delights. The righteousness of Your testimonies is everlasting. I pray that You will give her understanding, and she shall live.

PSALM 119:143–144

I pray that in righteousness my grandchild shall be established. That she shall be far from oppression, for she shall not fear; and from terror, for it shall not come near her.

ISAIAH 54:14

I pray that it is good for my grandchild that she has been afflicted so that she may learn from Your statutes.

PSALM 119:71

I pray that You, God, will consider my grand-child's affliction and deliver her, for she does not forget Your law. I pray that You will plead her cause and redeem her. Revive her according to Your word.

PSALM 119:153–154

I pray that my grandchild has great peace because she loves Your law, God, and nothing causes her to stumble.

PSALM 119:165

I pray that if my grandchild has gone astray like a lost sheep; that You, God, will seek her, Your ser-vant, and not let her forget Your commandments.

PSALM 119:176

13

DON'T UNDERSTAND GOD

Lord God, the words that I am about to pray are Your words. Hear them please and honor them. Help my grandchild to understand that because Your thoughts are often higher than his thoughts, he may not always understand Your thoughts and Your way. Remind him of Your promise that if he will call upon You, You will tell him great and unsearchable things that he does not know. In Jesus' name. Amen.

**God, in accordance
with Your word . . .**

I pray that You, God, will help my grandchild to understand that Your thoughts are not his thoughts, nor are his ways Your ways. That he will understand that as the heavens are higher than the earth, so are Your ways higher than his ways, and Your thoughts higher than his thoughts.

ISAIAH 55:8–9

I pray that my grandchild will call to You, God, and that You will answer him and show him great and mighty things, which he does not know.

JEREMIAH 33:3

---✽---

I pray that if You, God, are for my grandchild, who can be against him?

ROMANS 8:31

---✽---

I pray that in all things my grandchild is more than a conqueror through Him who loved him.

ROMANS 8:37

---✽---

I pray that as for You, God, Your way is perfect. The word of the LORD is proven; You are a shield to my grandchild who trusts in You.

PSALM 18:30

I pray that my grandchild will pursue the knowledge of the LORD.

HOSEA 6:3

---- ❀ ----

I pray, God, that You will perfect that which concerns my grandchild and that Your mercy, O LORD, endures forever.

PSALM 138:8

---- ❀ ----

I pray that You, God, will make an everlasting covenant with my grandchild, that You will not turn away from doing him good; but that You will put Your fear in his heart so that he will not depart from You.

JEREMIAH 32:40

---- ❀ ----

I pray that my grandchild will hold fast the confession of his hope without wavering, for You, God, who promised are faithful.

HEBREWS 10:23

14
DOUBTING GOD

Heavenly Father, today I pray the power of Your perfect words to remove any doubts about You that my grandchild might have. Your words say that Your way is perfect, and Your words are proven. Use Your Holy Spirit to impart Your perfection to my grandchild and to remove any doubts that she may have now or at any time in her life. Help her more than ever before to believe and not doubt. And it is in Jesus' name that I pray. Amen.

God, in accordance
with Your word . . .

I pray that because Your way is perfect and Your word is proven; that You, God, are a shield to all who trust in You.

PSALM 18:30

I pray, God, that my grandchild will always re-member that Your hand is not shortened so that it cannot save; nor Your ear heavy, that it cannot hear.

ISAIAH 59:1

I pray that You, Lord, are not slack concerning Your promise, as some count slackness, but are longsuffering toward my grandchild, not willing that she should perish but that she should come to repentance.

2 PETER 3:9

I pray, God, that my grandchild is aware that You have said Your counsel shall stand, and You will do all Your pleasure. Indeed, You have spoken it and You will also bring it to pass. You have purposed it and You will also do it.

ISAIAH 46:10–11

I pray that my grandchild knows that He who calls her is faithful, who also will do it.

1 THESSALONIANS 5:24

I pray that my grandchild does not seek what she
should eat or what she should drink, nor have an
anxious mind. For all these things the nations of
the world seek after, and You, her Father, know
that she needs these things. I pray that she will
seek the kingdom of God, and all these things
shall be added to her.

LUKE 12:29–31

I pray that my grandchild will always remember
that You, God, have declared that, "So shall My
word be that goes forth from My mouth; it shall
not return to Me void, but it shall accomplish
what I please, and it shall prosper in the thing for
which I sent it."

ISAIAH 55:11

15
EMOTIONALLY UPSET

Jesus, I am here to pray Your words and to ask You to give great peace to my grandchild because he loves You so much. As Your words say, give him a sound mind and a peace that passes all understanding. In accordance with Your words, let him be anxious for nothing. Thank You, Jesus, for honoring Your words in this important time in my grandchild's life. Amen.

God, in accordance
with Your word . . .

I pray that my grandchild will have great peace because he loves Your law, and nothing causes him to stumble.

PSALM 119:165

I pray that because my grandchild believes in You, God, he will by no means be put to shame.

1 PETER 2:6

I pray that You, God, will help my grandchild; there-fore he will not be disgraced. He can set his face like a flint and know that he will not be ashamed.

ISAIAH 50:7

I pray that my grandchild will be anxious for noth-ing, but in everything by prayer and supplication, with thanksgiving, will let his requests be made known to You, God; and Your peace, God, which surpasses all understanding, will guard his heart and mind through Christ Jesus.

PHILIPPIANS 4:6–7

I pray that my grandchild will cast his burden on You, LORD, and that You shall sustain him.

PSALM 55:22

I pray that You, God, have not given my grand-child a spirit of fear, but of power and of love and of a sound mind.

2 TIMOTHY 1:7

I pray that my grandchild will fear not, for You, God, are with him. That he be not dismayed, for You are his God. I pray that You will strengthen him and help him and that You will uphold him with Your righteous right hand.

ISAIAH 41:10

I pray that my grandchild knows that where envy and self-seeking exist, confusion and every evil thing will be there. I pray that he will also know that the wisdom that is from above is first pure, then peaceable, gentle, willing to yield, full of mercy and good fruits, without partiality and without hypocrisy and that the fruit of righteousness is sown in peace by those who make peace.

JAMES 3:16–18

16

FAITH

Father God, in the name of Your Son, Jesus, I pray to You Your perfect words for my grandchild. Increase her faith. Help her to remember that You said she is to walk by faith and not by sight. Hear and answer Your words now concerning my grandchild's faith. Thank You in Jesus' name. Amen.

**God, in accordance
with Your word . . .**

I pray that You, Lord, will increase my grandchild's faith.

LUKE 17:5

I pray that my grandchild's faith comes by hearing, and hearing by the word of God.

ROMANS 10:17

I pray that my grandchild will walk by faith and not by sight.

2 CORINTHIANS 5:7

I pray that my grandchild will have a pure heart, a good conscience and sincere faith.

1 TIMOTHY 1:5

I pray that my grandchild will always remember that faith is the substance of things hoped for and the evidence of things not seen.

HEBREWS 11:1

I pray that my grandchild remembers that faith by itself, if it does not have works, is dead.

JAMES 2:17

I pray that my grandchild will constantly take the shield of faith with which she will be able to quench all the fiery darts of the wicked one.

EPHESIANS 6:16

I pray that my grandchild will put on the breast-plate of faith and love, and as her helmet the hope of salvation.

1 THESSALONIANS 5:8

I pray that my grandchild will always have faith and a good conscience.

1 TIMOTHY 1:19

I pray that my grandchild will fight the good fight of faith, that she will lay hold on eternal life, to which she was also called.

1 TIMOTHY 6:12

17

FEAR

God, I pray Your words to You to remove any and all fears that my grandchild may be harboring now or in the future. I ask You to remember that my prayers are actually Your words on the subject of fear. Please honor Your perfect and error-free words and remove any and all fears now and forever in my grandchild. Thank You, God, for hearing my prayers. In Jesus' name. Amen.

God, in accordance
with Your word . . .

I pray that Your truth, God, shall be my grand-child's shield and buckler and that he shall not be afraid.

PSALM 91:4–5

I pray that no evil shall befall my grandchild.

PSALM 91:10

I pray that my grandchild will not be afraid of sudden terror, nor of trouble from the wicked when it comes. I pray that You, LORD, will be his confidence and will keep his foot from being caught.

PROVERBS 3:25–26

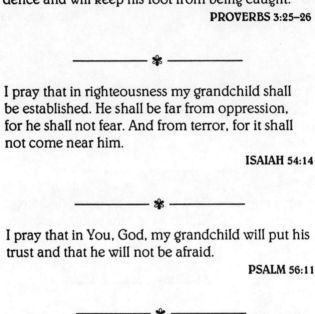

I pray that in righteousness my grandchild shall be established. He shall be far from oppression, for he shall not fear. And from terror, for it shall not come near him.

ISAIAH 54:14

I pray that in You, God, my grandchild will put his trust and that he will not be afraid.

PSALM 56:11

I pray that my grandchild knows that You, God, have not given him a spirit of fear, but of power and of love and of a sound mind.

2 TIMOTHY 1:7

I pray that my grandchild did not receive the spirit of bondage again to fear, but that he received the Spirit of adoption by whom he cries out, "Abba, Father."

ROMANS 8:15

———— ❈ ————

I pray that in my grandchild there is no fear in love; because perfect love casts out fear.

1 JOHN 4:18

———— ❈ ————

I pray that You, God, will give Your angels charge over my grandchild, to keep him in all his ways.

PSALM 91:11

———— ❈ ————

I pray that though my grandchild walks through the valley of the shadow of death, he will fear no evil; for You, God, are with him. Your rod and Your staff, they comfort him.

PSALM 23:4

18
FINANCIAL PROBLEMS

Heavenly Father, it is not Your will that my grand-child should have to contend unnecessarily with financial problems. Because I believe strongly in Your words, I present to You as my prayers for my grandchild Your very words on this subject. Please honor Your words, and release her from any and all financial problems in her life. I pray Your words in Jesus' name. Amen.

**God, in accordance
with Your word . . .**

I pray that my grandchild may prosper in all things and be in health, just as her soul prospers.

3 JOHN 1:2

I pray that You, LORD, are my grandchild's shep-herd and that she shall not want.

PSALM 23:1

I pray that my grandchild will seek You, LORD, and not lack any good thing.

PSALM 34:10

I pray that all these blessings shall come upon my grandchild and overtake her, because she obeys the voice of the LORD, her God. She shall be blessed in the city and she shall be blessed in the country. She shall be blessed when she comes in and she shall be blessed when she goes out. I pray that You, LORD, will command Your blessing on her in her storehouses and in all to which she sets her hand.

DEUTERONOMY 28:2–3, 6, 8

I pray that my grandchild will give, and it will be given to her: good measure, pressed down, shaken together, and running over will be put into her bosom. For with the same measure that she uses, it will be measured back to her.

LUKE 6:38

I pray that because freely my grandchild has received, freely she will give.

MATTHEW 10:8

---- ❀ ----

I pray that on the first day of the week my grandchild will lay something aside, storing up as she may prosper, so that there be no collections when it is time to give.

1 CORINTHIANS 16:2

---- ❀ ----

I pray that my grandchild will bring all her tithes into the storehouse, that there may be food in God's house. And that she will try You, God, in this and see if You will not open for her the windows of heaven and pour out for her such blessing that there will not be room enough to receive it.

MALACHI 3:10

---- ❀ ----

I pray that my grandchild leaves an inheritance to her children's children.

PROVERBS 13:22

19
FORGIVENESS

Lord God, for reasons known to You, my grandchild needs Your forgiveness. Because I sense that and know that he has need of Your forgiveness, I come to You today, praying that he might be forgiven. Bless now Your very words on my grandchild's behalf. Thank You now in Jesus' name. Amen.

**God, in accordance
with Your word . . .**

I pray that as far as the east is from the west, so far have You, God, removed my grandchild's transgressions from him.

PSALM 103:12

I pray that it is You who blots out my grandchild's transgressions for Your own sake and that You will not remember his sins.

ISAIAH 43:25

I pray that my grandchild will return to You, LORD, and that You will have mercy on him; and to his God, for You will abundantly pardon.

ISAIAH 55:7

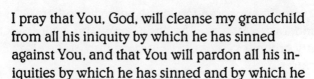

I pray that You, God, will cleanse my grandchild from all his iniquity by which he has sinned against You, and that You will pardon all his iniquities by which he has sinned and by which he has transgressed against You.

JEREMIAH 33:8

I pray that whenever my grandchild stands praying, if he has anything against anyone that he will forgive him, so that You, his Father in heaven, may also forgive him of his trespasses.

MARK 11:25

I pray that my grandchild's transgressions are forgiven and his sin is covered.

PSALM 32:1

I pray that in You, Jesus, my grandchild has redemption through Your blood, the forgiveness of his sins, according to the riches of God's grace.

EPHESIANS 1:7–9

I pray that my grandchild will bear with others, and forgive others, if he has a complaint against any others; even as Christ forgave him, so he also must do.

COLOSSIANS 3:13

I pray that my grandchild will walk by faith and not by sight.

2 CORINTHIANS 5:7

20
GODLY LIFE

Lord Jesus, my Lord and my Savior, more than anything else I desire that my wonderful grandchild will live a godly life in Your sight. Your words are my prayers to You on her behalf. Please honor them by keeping my grandchild in the center of Your will in all that she does. Thank You for all that You do and especially for honoring this my prayer. Amen.

God, in accordance
with Your word . . .

I pray that if my grandchild lives, she lives to You, Lord; and if she dies, she dies to You, Lord. Therefore, whether she lives or dies, she is Yours, Lord.

ROMANS 14:8

I pray that if my grandchild believes on You, Jesus, who justifies the ungodly, her faith is accounted for righteousness.

ROMANS 4:5

I pray that what the law could not do in my grandchild in that it was weak through the flesh, You,
God, did by sending Your own Son in the likeness
of sinful flesh, on account of sin: You condemned
sin in my grandchild, that the righteous require-
ment of the law might be fulfilled in she who does
not walk according to the flesh but according to
the Spirit.

ROMANS 8:3–4

I pray that my grandchild does not present her
members as instruments of unrighteousness to
sin, but presents herself to You, God, as being
alive from the dead, and her members as instruments of righteousness to You. For sin shall not
have dominion over her, for she is not under law
but under grace.

ROMANS 6:13–14

I pray that my grandchild will present her body as
a living sacrifice, holy, acceptable to You, God.

ROMANS 12:1

I pray that my grandchild will not be conformed to this world, but that she will be transformed by the renewing of her mind, that she may prove what is that good and acceptable and perfect will of God.

ROMANS 12:2

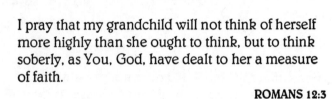

I pray that my grandchild will not think of herself more highly than she ought to think, but to think soberly, as You, God, have dealt to her a measure of faith.

ROMANS 12:3

I pray that because You, Christ, are in my grandchild, her body is dead because of sin, but the Spirit is life because of righteousness.

ROMANS 8:10

21

GOD'S LOVE

Lord God, I pray Your words to You as my way to ask You to love my grandchild in a very special way. Lord, help him to experience Your love through Your words and through other ways as well. Thank You, Father, in Jesus' name. Amen.

**God, in accordance
with Your word . . .**

I pray that my grandchild knows that love is not that he loved You, God, but that You loved him and sent Your Son to be the propitiation for his sins.

1 JOHN 4:10

---------- ❈ ----------

I pray that my grandchild loves You, God, because You first loved him.

1 JOHN 4:19

I pray that You, Christ, may dwell in my grandchild's heart through faith and that he, being
rooted and grounded in love, may be able to com-
prehend with all the saints what is the width and
length and depth and height—to know Your love
which passes knowledge; that he may be filled
with all the fullness of God.

EPHESIANS 3:17–19

I pray that my grandchild never forgets that You,
God, demonstrated Your own love toward him, in
that while he was still a sinner, Christ died for him.

ROMANS 5:8

I pray that You, God, so loved my grandchild that
You gave Your only begotten Son, that my grandchild who believes in Him should not perish but
have everlasting life.

JOHN 3:16

I pray that my grandchild has Your commandments, Jesus, and keeps them and loves You. And because he loves You he will be loved by God, and You will love him and manifest Yourself to him.

JOHN 14:21

I pray that my grandchild knows that You, God, have loved him with an everlasting love and with lovingkindness You have drawn him.

JEREMIAH 31:3

I pray that my grandchild realizes that You, God, will rejoice over him with gladness. That You will quiet him with Your love and that You will rejoice over him with singing.

ZEPHANIAH 3:17

22

GOD'S WORD

Heavenly Father, Your words are such an important part of my life. I pray that it will be the same in my grandchild's life and that Your words will be living and sharper than any two-edged sword in her life. I'm praying that Your words be important to her. Thank You, Father, in Jesus' name for hearing and answering my prayers for my grandchild. Amen.

**God, in accordance
with Your word . . .**

I pray, God, that in my grandchild's life Your word is living and powerful, and sharper than any two-edged sword, piercing even to the division of her soul and spirit, and of her joints and marrow, and that it is a discerner of the thoughts and intents of her heart.

HEBREWS 4:12

I pray that my grandchild has been born again, not of corruptible seed but incorruptible, through Your word, God, which lives and abides forever.

1 PETER 1:23

I pray that my grandchild never forgets that the word of the LORD endures forever.

1 PETER 1:25

I pray that my grandchild puts into practice the fact that she shall not live by bread alone, but by every word that proceeds from the mouth of God.

MATTHEW 4:4

I pray that my grandchild will always understand and apply the fact that all Scripture is given by Your inspiration, God, and is profitable for doctrine, for reproof, for correction, for instruction in righteousness, that she may be complete, thoroughly equipped for every good work.

2 TIMOTHY 3:16–17

I pray that my grandchild knows that she has been given exceedingly great and precious promises, that through these she may be a partaker of the divine nature, having escaped the corruption that is in the world through lust.

2 PETER 1:4

I pray that my grandchild always remembers that heaven and earth will pass away, but Jesus' words will by no means pass away.

MATTHEW 24:35

I pray that my grandchild understands the significance of the fact that until heaven and earth pass away, one jot or one tittle will by no means pass from the law till all is fulfilled.

MATTHEW 5:18

23
GRIEF/HURTING

God, You know the hurt in my grandchild's life. And You already know other hurts that are yet to come to him. By and through Your words, I pray that You will console my grandchild in a very special way. Wipe away his tears, and bring joy back into his life. I pray Your own words for those results. Please hear and honor them in Jesus' name. Amen.

**God, in accordance
with Your word . . .**

I pray that You, God, will console my grandchild who mourns and give him beauty for ashes, the oil of joy for mourning, the garment of praise for the spirit of heaviness so that he may be called a tree of righteousness.

ISAIAH 61:3

I pray that my grandchild is blessed when he mourns for he shall be comforted.

MATTHEW 5:4

I pray, O God, that You will comfort my grandchild in all his tribulations, that he may be able to comfort those who are in any trouble, with the comfort with which he himself is comforted by You.

2 CORINTHIANS 1:4

I pray that my grandchild will not be ignorant concerning those who have fallen asleep, lest he sorrow as others who have no hope.

1 THESSALONIANS 4:13

I pray, O God, that You have comforted my grandchild and will have mercy on his affliction.

ISAIAH 49:13

I pray that the Lord Jesus Christ Himself and You, God, who have loved my grandchild and given him everlasting consolation and good hope by grace, will comfort his heart and establish him in every good word and work.

2 THESSALONIANS 2:16–17

I pray that my grandchild always remembers that in You, Jesus, he does not have a High Priest who cannot sympathize with his weaknesses, but was in all points tempted as he is, yet without sin. Let him therefore come boldly to the throne of grace, that he may obtain mercy and find grace to help in time of need.

HEBREWS 4:15–16

I pray that in this crucial time in my grandchild's life he can say, "O Death, where is your sting? O Hades, where is your victory?"

1 CORINTHIANS 15:55

24

INHERITANCE

Lord God, in Your Son's name and through Your perfect words, I pray that my grandchild will be fully aware of and never forget the magnitude of the inheritance that awaits her. Give her a vision of that inheritance as even now I pray Your words for her. Thank You, God, in Jesus' name. Amen.

**God, in accordance
with Your word . . .**

I pray that whatever my grandchild does, she will do it heartily, as to You, Lord, and not to men, knowing that from You she will receive the reward of the inheritance; for she serves the Lord Christ.

COLOSSIANS 3:23–24

I pray that my grandchild has an inheritance in-

corruptible and undefiled and that does not fade
away, reserved in heaven for her.

1 PETER 1:4

I pray that my grandchild has been given exceedingly great and precious promises, that through
these she may be a partaker of the divine nature,
having escaped the corruption that is in the world
through lust.

2 PETER 1:4

I commend my grandchild to You, God, and to
the word of Your grace, which is able to build her
up and give her an inheritance among all those
who are sanctified.

ACTS 20:32

I pray, God, that the Spirit Himself bears witness
with my spirit that my grandchild is a child of
Yours and if a child, then an heir—an heir of
Yours and a joint heir with Christ, if indeed she

suffers with Him, that she may also be glorified together with Him.

ROMANS 8:16–17

I pray that my grandchild in You, Jesus, has obtained an inheritance, being predestined according to the purpose of Him who works all things according to the counsel of His will, that she who first trusted in You should be to the praise of His glory. In You, Jesus, she also trusted, after she heard the word of truth, the gospel of her salvation; in whom also, having believed, she was sealed with the Holy Spirit of promise, who is the guarantee of our inheritance until the redemption of the purchased possession, to the praise of His glory.

EPHESIANS 1:11–14

I pray, Lord, that my grandchild is aware that eye has not seen, nor ear heard, nor have entered into her heart the things which You have prepared for those who love You.

1 CORINTHIANS 2:9

25

LONELY

Jesus, I pray to You concerning any feeling of being lonely that my grandchild may be experiencing now or may experience in the future. As I pray Your words, help him to remember that You said that You would be with him always and that You are his constant companion. I pray Your very words to this end. In Your name I pray. Amen.

**God, in accordance
with Your word . . .**

I pray that my grandchild's conduct will be without covetousness, and that he will be content with such things as he has. For You, God, said, "I will never leave you nor forsake you."

HEBREWS 13:5

———— ✻ ————

I pray that my grandchild remembers Jesus' promise to be with him always, even to the end of the age.

MATTHEW 28:20

I pray that my grandchild will fear not, for You, God, are with him. That he be not dismayed, for You are his God. I pray that You will strengthen him and that You will help him and that You will uphold him with Your righteous right hand.

ISAIAH 41:10

I pray that my grandchild realizes that You, God, count the number of the stars and call them all by name. I pray that he remembers that great is his Lord and mighty in power and that Your understanding is infinite.

PSALM 147:4–5

I pray, God, that neither death nor life, nor angels nor principalities nor powers, nor things present nor things to come, nor height nor depth, nor any other created thing, shall be able to separate my grandchild from Your love, God, which is in Christ Jesus his Lord.

ROMANS 8:38–39

I pray, Jesus, that my grandchild remembers Your promise that You will not leave him as an orphan but that You will come to him.

JOHN 14:18

I pray that my grandchild will be strong and of good courage and that he does not fear nor is he afraid of them, for You, the LORD, his God, You are the One who goes with him. I pray that You will not leave him nor forsake him.

DEUTERONOMY 31:6

I pray that if my grandchild's father and his mother forsake him, then You, LORD, will take care of him.

PSALM 27:10

26

LOVE

God, Your words tell us that You are love and that we must love others even as You have loved us. This is such an important matter that I want now to pray Your very words on my grandchild's behalf. Honor Your words, Lord, as my prayers for my grandchild. Thank You for the privilege of praying in Jesus' name. Amen.

God, in accordance with Your word . . .

I pray that my grandchild will love others, for love is of You, God.

1 JOHN 4:7

I pray that my grandchild understands the true meaning of love and that though she speaks with the tongues of men and of angels, but has not love, she has become sounding brass or a clanging cymbal. And though she has the gift of prophecy, and understands all mysteries and all knowledge, and though she has all faith, so that she can remove mountains, but has not love, she is nothing. And though she bestows all her goods to feed the poor, and though she gives her body to be burned, but has not love, it profits her nothing. I pray that she remembers that love suffers long and is kind; love does not envy; love does not parade itself, is not puffed up; does not behave rudely, does not seek its own, is not provoked, thinks no evil; does not rejoice in iniquity, but rejoices in the truth; bears all things, believes all things, hopes all things, endures all things. Help her to understand that love never fails. Help her to abide in faith, hope, love, these three; but the greatest of these is love.

1 CORINTHIANS 13:1–8, 13

I pray that my grandchild understands that love is not that she loved You, God, but that You loved her and sent Your Son to be the propitiation for her sins. And help her to know that if You so loved her, she also ought to love others.

1 JOHN 4:10–11

I pray that my grandchild totally understands that as You, God, loved Jesus, He also has loved her and she is to abide in His love.

JOHN 15:9

I pray that if my grandchild has Jesus' commandments and keeps them, it is she who loves Him. And my grandchild who loves Jesus will be loved by You, God, and Jesus will love her and manifest Himself to her.

JOHN 14:21

I pray, God, that You have loved my grandchild with an everlasting love and with lovingkindness have drawn her to You.

JEREMIAH 31:3

I pray that You, God, love my grandchild, because she has loved Jesus, and has believed that He came forth from You.

JOHN 16:27

27

LOVE FOR MY GRANDCHILD

Lord, I pray these Your words for my grandchild. Honor my prayers by honoring Your own words. I praise You and pray to You in Jesus' name. Amen.

God, in accordance
with Your word . . .

I pray that while my grandchild and I have not seen You, God, at any time, if we love one another, You abide in us, and Your love has been perfected in us.

1 JOHN 4:12

I pray, Jesus, that my grandchild and I will follow Your commandment that we love one another as You have loved us.

JOHN 15:12

I pray that if You, God, so loved my grandchild
and me, we also ought to love one another.

1 JOHN 4:11

---- ❀ ----

I pray, Lord Jesus, that by this my grandchild and I
know love, because You laid down Your life for
us. And we also ought to lay down our lives for
each other.

1 JOHN 3:16

---- ❀ ----

I pray, Lord God, that my grandchild and I will
love one another, for love is of You; and everyone
who loves is born of You and knows You. But if
we do not love we do not know You, for You are
love.

1 JOHN 4:7–8

---- ❀ ----

I pray, Jesus, that my grandchild and I will follow
Your command that we love one another.

JOHN 15:17

I pray, Lord Jesus, that my grandchild and I always remember that when we were still without strength, in due time You died for us.

ROMANS 5:6

I pray that my grandchild and I will always understand the significance of the question, "Can two walk together, unless they are agreed?"

AMOS 3:3

28
NEEDS

Lord, You and You alone know all of my grandchild's needs. I desire now to spend time with You praying for her needs. I ask You to bless the praying of Your words and to honor Your words by meeting my grandchild's needs. I pray in Jesus' name. Amen.

**God, in accordance
with Your word . . .**

I pray that my grandchild will delight herself also in You, LORD, and that You will give her the desires of her heart.

PSALM 37:4

I pray that You, LORD, will guide my grandchild continually.

ISAIAH 58:11

I pray that my grandchild will not spend wages for what does not satisfy and that she will listen carefully to You, God, and will let her soul delight itself in abundance.

ISAIAH 55:2

❊

I pray that whatever things my grandchild asks in prayer, believing, she will receive.

MATTHEW 21:22

❊

I pray, Jesus, that if my grandchild asks anything in Your name, You will do it.

JOHN 14:14

❊

I pray, Lord Jesus, that if my grandchild abides in You and Your words abide in her, she will ask what she desires, and it shall be done for her.

JOHN 15:7

I pray that my grandchild will ask in Your name,
Jesus, and she will receive, that her joy may be full.

JOHN 16:24

———————— �֍ ————————

I pray that my grandchild shall know the truth
and the truth shall make her free.

JOHN 8:32

———————— �֍ ————————

I pray that You, the God and Father of our Lord Jesus Christ, have blessed my grandchild with every
spiritual blessing in the heavenly places in Christ.

EPHESIANS 1:3

———————— ✖ ————————

I pray that my grandchild can do all things
through Christ who strengthens her.

PHILIPPIANS 4:13

29

OBEDIENCE

God, You have said that obedience is more important to You than sacrifice. Because I believe that You meant what You said, I now pray Your powerful words. God, in Jesus' name I ask You to help my grandchild be obedient to You in every way and in every situation. Having asked You for it in Jesus' name, I believe that it will happen, and I thank You in His name. Amen.

**God, in accordance
with Your word . . .**

I pray that my grandchild recognizes the fact that You, God, have set before him today a blessing and a curse: the blessing, if he obeys the commandments of the LORD his God which You have commanded him today; and the curse, if he does not obey the commandments of the LORD his God, but turns aside from the way which You

command him today, to go after other gods
which he has not known.

DEUTERONOMY 11:26–28

I pray that my grandchild never forgets that to
obey is better than sacrifice.

1 SAMUEL 15:22

I pray that my grandchild will heed Your commandments, O God, so that his peace will be like
a river and his righteousness like the waves of the
sea.

ISAIAH 48:18

I pray, O God, that my grandchild will obey Your
voice, and You will be his God, and he shall be
Your child. And that he will walk in all the ways
that You have commanded him, that it may be
well with him.

JEREMIAH 7:23

I pray, Lord Jesus, that my grandchild loves You
and keeps Your commandments.

JOHN 14:15

———————— ❊ ————————

I pray, God, that my grandchild knows that he
ought to obey You rather than men.

ACTS 5:29

———————— ❊ ————————

I pray, Jesus, that my grandchild will always keep
Your commandments.

1 JOHN 2:3

———————— ❊ ————————

I pray that my grandchild will walk in Your ways,
God, to keep Your statutes and Your commandments, and that You will lengthen his days.

1 KINGS 3:14

30

PATImage

Lord Jesus, patience is so important but so elusive. I pray to You now what You have already declared, and I ask You to honor my requests in my grandchild's life. Bless now the praying of Your words. Amen.

**God, in accordance
with Your word . . .**

I pray that whatever things were written for my grandchild's learning, that she through the patience and comfort of the Scriptures might have hope. Now may You, the God of patience and comfort, grant my grandchild to be like-minded toward others, according to Christ Jesus.

ROMANS 15:4–5

I pray that my grandchild will glory in tribulations, knowing that tribulation produces perseverance; and perseverance, character; and character, hope.

ROMANS 5:3–4

———————— ✾ ————————

I pray that my grandchild will rest in You, LORD, and that she will wait patiently for You. I pray that she does not fret because of he who prospers in her way, or because of the man who brings wicked schemes to pass. I pray that she will cease from anger, and forsake wrath, and that she does not fret—it only causes harm.

PSALM 37:7–8

———————— ✾ ————————

I pray that my grandchild will wait patiently for You, LORD, and that You will incline Yourself to her and hear her cry.

PSALM 40:1

———————— ✾ ————————

I pray that my grandchild will imitate those who through faith and patience inherit the promises.

HEBREWS 6:12

I pray that my grandchild does not cast away her confidence, which has great reward. For she has need of endurance, so that after she has done Your will, God, she may receive her promise.

HEBREWS 10:35–36

I pray that since my grandchild is surrounded by so great a cloud of witnesses, let her lay aside every weight, and the sin which so easily ensnares her, and let her run with endurance the race that is set before her.

HEBREWS 12:1

I pray that my grandchild will not hasten in her spirit to be angry, for anger rests in the bosom of fools.

ECCLESIASTES 7:9

31

PEACE

Heavenly Father, just as Your words say, I pray perfect peace for my grandchild. There is no process I know of that is more important to his having peace than to pray. It is Your words that I pray in Jesus' name, and I thank You for hearing and answering these my prayers. Amen.

**God, in accordance
with Your word . . .**

I pray, God, that You will keep my grandchild in perfect peace, whose mind is stayed on You, because he trusts in You.

ISAIAH 26:3

I pray that Your kindness, God, shall not depart from my grandchild, nor shall Your covenant of peace be removed from him.

ISAIAH 54:10

I pray that my grandchild will lie down in peace, and sleep; for You alone, O LORD, make him dwell in safety.

PSALM 4:8

I pray, O LORD, that You will give strength to my grandchild and that You will bless him with peace.

PSALM 29:11

I pray that You, Jesus, have left Your peace with my grandchild. I pray that his heart will not be troubled, neither will he be afraid.

JOHN 14:27

I pray that my grandchild who has been justified by faith, will have peace with You, God, through his Lord Jesus Christ.

ROMANS 5:1

I pray that Jesus Himself is my grandchild's peace.

EPHESIANS 2:14

I pray that my grandchild will be anxious for nothing, but in everything by prayer and supplication, with thanksgiving, will let his requests be made known to You, God; and Your peace which surpasses all understanding, will guard his heart and mind through Christ Jesus.

PHILIPPIANS 4:6–7

I pray, God, that the peace of God rule in my grandchild's heart.

COLOSSIANS 3:15

32

POWER

Lord God, my grandchild is in need of Your power. That power comes only through Your words, and that is what I pray to You today. Honor these prayers and bring Your power into the life of my grandchild. In the name of Jesus I offer up Your words for my grandchild. Thank You for hearing and answering each of these prayers. Amen.

**God, in accordance
with Your word . . .**

I pray that my grandchild will take pleasure in infirmities, in reproaches, in needs, in persecutions, in distresses, for Christ's sake. For when she is weak, then she is strong.

2 CORINTHIANS 12:10

I pray that in all things my grandchild is more than a conqueror through Jesus who loved her.

ROMANS 8:37

I pray that my grandchild can do all things through Christ who strengthens her.

PHILIPPIANS 4:13

I pray, Jesus, that whatever my grandchild asks in Your name that You will do, that the Father may be glorified in the Son.

JOHN 14:13

I pray that You, God, are able to make all grace abound toward my grandchild, that she, always having all sufficiency in all things, may have an abundance for every good work.

2 CORINTHIANS 9:8

I pray, Jesus, that Your grace is sufficient for my grandchild, for Your strength is made perfect in weakness.

2 CORINTHIANS 12:9

I pray that my grandchild will see the exceeding greatness of Your power, God, toward her who believes, according to the working of Your mighty power.

EPHESIANS 1:19

I pray, O God, that You are able to do exceedingly abundantly above all that my grandchild asks or thinks, according to the power that works in her.

EPHESIANS 3:20

33

PRAISE

Heavenly Father, we were created to praise You. Through the praying of Your words, I petition You to put into my grandchild's heart a consistent desire to praise You at all times. These words of Yours are my prayers in Jesus' name. Amen.

God, in accordance with Your word . . .

I pray, LORD God, that my grandchild will sing praises to You and that he will declare Your deeds among the people.

PSALM 9:11

I pray that my grandchild will sing praises to You, LORD, as long as he lives.

PSALM 104:33

I pray, O LORD, that my grandchild will praise You.

ISAIAH 12:1

———— ❋ ————

I pray that my grandchild will give You thanks, O
Lord God Almighty, the One who is and who was
and who is to come, because You have taken
Your great power and reigned.

REVELATION 11:17

———— ❋ ————

I pray that my grandchild will hope continually, O
God, and will praise You yet more and more.

PSALM 71:14

———— ❋ ————

I pray, God, that my grandchild will enter into
Your gates with thanksgiving and into Your courts
with praise.

PSALM 100:4

———— ❋ ————

I pray that You, LORD, are my grandchild's

strength and song and that You have become his salvation; that You are his God, and that he will praise You.

EXODUS 15:2

------ ❊ ------

I pray that my grandchild will proclaim the name of the LORD and ascribe greatness to You his God.

DEUTERONOMY 32:3

------ ❊ ------

I pray that my grandchild will proclaim, "The LORD lives! Blessed be my Rock! Let God be exalted, the Rock of my salvation!"

2 SAMUEL 22:47

------ ❊ ------

I pray that my grandchild always remembers that You, LORD, are great and greatly to be praised.

1 CHRONICLES 16:25

34

PROTECTION

Lord God, honor the prayers I lift up to You for my grandchild's protection. They are Your words straight from the Bible. Protect her at all times through Jesus' name. Amen.

**God, in accordance
with Your word . . .**

I pray that my grandchild's LORD God, who goes before her, will fight for her.

DEUTERONOMY 1:30

I pray that if my grandchild will indeed obey Your voice, God, and do all that You speak, then You will be an enemy to her enemies and an adversary to her adversaries.

EXODUS 23:22

I pray that no weapon formed against my grand-child shall prosper, and every tongue which rises against her in judgment, You, God, shall condemn.

ISAIAH 54:17

---- ❀ ----

I pray that Jesus has given my grandchild the authority to trample on serpents and scorpions, and over all the power of the enemy, and nothing shall by any means hurt her.

LUKE 10:19

---- ❀ ----

I pray that You, Lord, are faithful, who will establish my grandchild and guard her from the evil one.

2 THESSALONIANS 3:3

---- ❀ ----

I pray that if God is for my grandchild, who can be against her?

ROMANS 8:31

35
REBELLIOUS

Lord God, through the power of Your words, I pray that no spirit of rebellion will ever enter into my grandchild. Through the praying of Your words, keep him free from any rebellious spirit or attitude. I pray to You, and I thank You in Jesus' precious name. Amen.

God, in accordance with Your word . . .

I pray that my grandchild, by doing good, may put to silence the ignorance of foolish men.

1 PETER 2:15

———— ✽ ————

I pray that if my grandchild is willing and obedient he shall eat the good of the land.

ISAIAH 1:19

I pray that my grandchild will gird up the loins of his mind, be sober, and rest his hope fully upon the grace that is to be brought to him at the revelation of Jesus Christ; as an obedient child, not conforming himself to the former lusts, as in his ignorance; but as You, God, who called him are holy, he also is to be holy in all his conduct.

1 PETER 1:13–15

I pray that my grandchild is aware that rebellion is as the sin of witchcraft.

1 SAMUEL 15:23

I pray that my grandchild will obey those who rule over him, and be submissive, for they watch out for his soul, as those who must give account.

HEBREWS 13:17

I pray that my grandchild will be like Jesus and humble himself and become obedient.

PHILIPPIANS 2:8

I pray that like You, Jesus, my grandchild learns obedience by the things which he suffers.

HEBREWS 5:8

I pray, God, that my grandchild knows that You resist the proud, but give grace to the humble and that he will humble himself under Your mighty hand, that You, God, may exalt him in due time.

1 PETER 5:5–6

I pray that my grandchild knows and understands that no grave trouble will overtake the righteous, but the wicked shall be filled with evil.

PROVERBS 12:21

I pray that my grandchild will submit to You, God; that he will resist the devil, and the devil will flee from him.

JAMES 4:7

I pray that while my grandchild was once darkness, now he is light in the Lord and that he will
walk as a child of the light.

EPHESIANS 5:8

I pray that my grandchild does not let sin reign in
his mortal body, that he should obey it in its lusts.
I also pray that he does not present himself to sin,
but that he presents himself to You, God, as being
alive from the dead, and his members as instruments of righteousness to God. For sin shall not
have dominion over him, for he is not under law
but under grace.

ROMANS 6:12–14

36
SALVATION

Lord, the most important thing in life is salvation. I pray for my grandchild's salvation through the powerful praying of Your holy words. Hear these my prayers for my grandchild. Honor them. And bless them with Your salvation. In Jesus' name I pray. Amen.

**God, in accordance
with Your word . . .**

I pray that my grandchild will discover that Jesus said, "He who believes in Me has everlasting life."

JOHN 6:47

I pray that my grandchild remembers that Jesus has come to seek and to save that which was lost.

LUKE 19:10

I pray, Lord Jesus, that my grandchild will come to understand what You meant when You said, "Therefore whoever confesses Me before men, him I will also confess before My Father who is in heaven."

MATTHEW 10:32

I pray that if my grandchild will confess with her mouth the Lord Jesus and believe in her heart that God raised Him from the dead, she will be saved. For with her heart she believes to righteousness, and with her mouth confession is made to salvation.

ROMANS 10:9–10

I pray that You, God, so loved my grandchild that You gave Your only begotten Son, that if my grandchild believes in Him she should not perish but have everlasting life.

JOHN 3:16

I pray that You did not send Your Son into the world to condemn my grandchild, but that my grandchild through Him might be saved.

JOHN 3:17

I pray that this will be my grandchild's testimony: that You, God, have given her eternal life, and this life is in Your Son.

1 JOHN 5:11

I pray that by grace my grandchild has been saved through faith, and not of herself; it is the gift of God, not of works, lest she should boast.

EPHESIANS 2:8–9

I pray that You, God, have saved my grandchild and called her with a holy calling, not according to her works, but according to Your own purpose and grace which was given to her in Christ Jesus before time began.

2 TIMOTHY 1:9

I pray, God, that it is not by works of righteousness which my grandchild has done, but according to Your mercy You saved her, through the
washing of regeneration and renewing of the Holy
Spirit whom You poured out on her abundantly
through Jesus Christ her Savior.

TITUS 3:5–6

I pray, God, that Jesus stands at the door and
knocks, and if my grandchild hears His voice and
opens the door, He will come in to her and dine
with her, and she with Him.

REVELATION 3:20

I pray, God, that my grandchild has been born
again, not of corruptible seed but incorruptible,
through Your word which lives and abides forever.

1 PETER 1:23

37
SATAN DEFEATED

Heavenly Father, my grandchild's enemy is Satan. Satan wants to destroy him. But God, Your words are stronger than Satan, and that is what I pray on my grandchild's behalf. I pray Your words that my grandchild will defeat every attack of Satan in his life. Thank You, God, in the powerful name of Jesus. Amen.

**God, in accordance
with Your word . . .**

I pray that my grandchild will be strong in You, Lord, and the power of Your might. I pray that he will put on the whole armor of God, that he may be able to stand against the wiles of the devil. For he does not wrestle against flesh and blood, but against principalities, against powers, against the rulers of the darkness of this age, against spiritual hosts of wickedness in the heavenly places. I pray that he will take up Your whole armor God, that he may be able to withstand in the evil day, and having done all, to stand. I pray that he has girded his waist with truth, having put on the breastplate of righteousness, and having shod his feet with the preparation of the gospel of peace and above all, taking the shield of faith with which he will be able to quench all the fiery darts of the wicked one. I pray that he also takes the helmet of salvation, and the sword of the Spirit, which is the word of God; praying always with all prayer and supplication in the Spirit, being watchful to this end with all perseverance and supplication for all the saints.

EPHESIANS 6:10–18

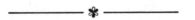

I pray that You, God, will open my grandchild's eyes, in order to turn them from darkness to light, and from the power of Satan to You, that he may receive forgiveness of sins and an inheritance among those who are sanctified by faith in Jesus.

ACTS 26:18

I pray, God, that You preserve the soul of my

grandchild and deliver him out of the hand of the wicked.

PSALM 97:10

I pray, God, for my grandchild that the Son of God was manifested that He might destroy the works of the devil.

1 JOHN 3:8

I pray for my grandchild that he puts off, concerning his former conduct, the old man which grows corrupt according to the deceitful lusts, and be renewed in the spirit of his mind and that he put on the new man which was created according to You, God, in true righteousness and holiness.

EPHESIANS 4:22–24

38
SECURITY

Lord, real and true security comes only from You. I
pray Your words concerning security for my grandchild. Through the praying of Your words help her
to sense the security that only You can give. Lord, I
thank You, and I pray in Your name. Amen.

**God, in accordance
with Your word . . .**

I pray that my grandchild is persuaded that neither death nor life, nor angels nor principalities
nor powers, nor things present nor things to
come, nor height nor depth, nor any other created thing, shall be able to separate her from the
love of God which is in Christ Jesus, her Lord.

ROMANS 8:38–39

I pray that in Jesus my grandchild also trusted, after she heard the word of truth, the gospel of her

salvation, in whom also, having believed, she was sealed with the Holy Spirit of promise.

EPHESIANS 1:13

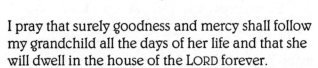

I pray that surely goodness and mercy shall follow my grandchild all the days of her life and that she will dwell in the house of the LORD forever.

PSALM 23:6

I pray that my grandchild is one of those who has come to You, Jesus, and who You will by no means cast out.

JOHN 6:37

I pray, Jesus, that my grandchild has heard Your voice and that You know her, and that she follows You and that You will give her eternal life, and she shall never perish.

JOHN 10:27-28

I pray that my grandchild does not grieve the Holy Spirit of God, by whom she was sealed for the day of redemption.

EPHESIANS 4:30

I pray that You, God, who have begun a good work in my grandchild will complete it until the day of Jesus Christ.

PHILIPPIANS 1:6

I pray, Lord, that Your faithfulness will establish my grandchild and guard her from the evil one.

2 THESSALONIANS 3:3

I pray that You, God, are able to keep my grandchild from stumbling and to present her faultless before the presence of Your glory with exceeding joy.

JUDE 1:24

39

SERVING GOD

Lord God, in accordance with Your perfect words, I pray that my grandchild will walk after You and that he will serve You. Your words are clear that he cannot serve two masters. Now—at this very moment—I ask You to honor Your words in the area of my grandchild's service to You. Use Your Holy Spirit to guide him and direct him in this area of his life in accordance with Your words which I now pray. Thank You in Jesus' name. Amen.

**God, in accordance
with Your word . . .**

I pray that my grandchild will walk after You, the LORD, his God, and fear You, and keep Your commandments and obey Your voice, and that he shall serve You and hold fast to You.

DEUTERONOMY 13:4

I pray that my grandchild will worship You, the Lord, his God, and You only he shall serve.

MATTHEW 4:10

I pray, God, that my grandchild knows that he cannot serve two masters; for either he will hate the one and love the other, or else he will be loyal to the one and despise the other. He cannot serve You and mammon.

MATTHEW 6:24

I pray that my grandchild will love You, the LORD, his God, and walk in all Your ways, keeping Your commandments, and holding fast to You, and serving You with all his heart and with all his soul.

JOSHUA 22:5

I pray to You, God, that my grandchild will present his body a living sacrifice, holy, acceptable to You, which is his reasonable service. I pray also that he will not be conformed to this world, but be transformed by the renewing of his mind, that he may prove what is that good and acceptable and perfect will of Yours.

ROMANS 12:1–2

I pray that my grandchild will be kindly affectionate to others with brotherly love, in honor giving preference to others; not lagging in diligence, fervent in spirit, serving You, the Lord; rejoicing in hope, patient in tribulation, continuing steadfastly in prayer; distributing to the needs of the saints, given to hospitality.

ROMANS 12:10–13

I pray, O God, that my grandchild shall serve You, the LORD, his God.

EXODUS 23:25

40
SICKNESS

Heavenly Father, in accordance with the perfection of Your words, I pray that You will heal my grandchild of her affliction and restore her health. We need Your help and pray Your words for that important need to be met. It is in the powerful name of Jesus that I pray to You. Amen.

God, in accordance
with Your word . . .

I pray that You will heal my grandchild, O LORD, and she shall be healed. Save her and she shall be saved.

JEREMIAH 17:14

I pray, God, that You will restore health to my grandchild and heal her wounds.

JEREMIAH 30:17

I pray that my grandchild will diligently heed
Your voice, LORD God, and do what is right in
Your sight and give ear to Your commandments
and keep all Your statutes, and that You will put
no diseases on her.

EXODUS 15:26

I pray, O God, that Jesus was wounded for my
grandchild's transgressions and He was bruised for
her iniquities; and by His stripes she is healed.

ISAIAH 53:5

I pray that Jesus Himself bore my grandchild's sins
in His own body on the tree, and that my grandchild, having died to sin, might live for righteousness—by whose stripes she was healed.

1 PETER 2:24

I pray, God, that You heal all my grandchild's diseases and redeem her life from destruction.

PSALM 103:3–4

I pray that my grandchild may prosper in all
things and be in health, just as her soul prospers.

3 JOHN 1:2

I pray, O God, that my grandchild remembers
that Jesus healed every sickness and every disease
among the people.

MATTHEW 9:35

I pray, Jesus, that power goes out from You and
heals my grandchild.

LUKE 6:19

41
SPIRITUAL GROWTH

Lord Jesus, there is no more powerful prayer that I can pray than to pray directly from the pages of the Bible. That is what I now do as I pray for my grandchild's spiritual growth. I pray that he will take heed to himself and keep himself in accordance with Your words. Thank You for honoring Your words. Amen.

**God, in accordance
with Your word . . .**

I pray that my grandchild will beware, lest there be in him an evil heart of unbelief in departing from the living God. I pray that I will exhort him daily, while it is called "Today," lest he be hardened through the deceitfulness of sin.

HEBREWS 3:12–13

I pray that my grandchild does not forget You, the

LORD, his God, by not keeping Your commandments, Your judgments, and Your statutes which
You command him today. I pray that he shall remember the LORD, his God, for it is You who gives
him the power to get wealth.

DEUTERONOMY 8:11, 18

I pray that my grandchild has not forgotten the
name of his God, or stretched out his hands to a
foreign god. Would You, God, not search this out?
For You know the secrets of the heart.

PSALM 44:20–21

I pray, God, that my grandchild will be watchful,
and strengthen the things which remain, that are
ready to die, for he has not found his works perfect before You.

REVELATION 3:2

I pray that my grandchild will take heed to himself, and diligently keep himself, lest he forget the

things his eyes have seen, and lest they depart
from his heart all the days of his life.

DEUTERONOMY 4:9

I pray, God, that my grandchild returns to You,
and You will return to him.

MALACHI 3:7

I pray that my grandchild will look diligently lest
he fall short of Your grace, God, and lest any root
of bitterness spring up causing trouble, and by this
he becomes defiled.

HEBREWS 12:15

I pray that after my grandchild has escaped the
pollution of the world through the knowledge of
his Lord and Savior, Jesus Christ, that he not become entangled in them and overcome.

2 PETER 2:20

42
STRENGTH

God, I call upon You now to give my grandchild more strength than ever before. I pray that You will increase her strength according to Your words, and I ask You to do that even as I pray Your words for strength for my grandchild. In Jesus' precious name I pray. Amen.

**God, in accordance
with Your word . . .**

I pray, God, that You give power to my grandchild, who is weak, and that You increase her strength.

ISAIAH 40:29

------------- ❋ -------------

I pray that my grandchild shall wait on You, LORD, and that she shall renew her strength. I pray that she shall mount up with wings like eagles, that she

shall run and not be weary and that she shall walk
and not faint.

ISAIAH 40:31

I pray that my grandchild will fear not, for You
are with her. I pray that she will be not dismayed,
for You are her God. You will strengthen her and
help her and You will uphold her with Your righteous right hand

ISAIAH 41:10

I pray that You, LORD, are my grandchild's rock
and her fortress and her deliverer; her God, her
strength, in whom she will trust; her shield and
the horn of her salvation, her stronghold. I pray
that she will call upon You, LORD, who are worthy
to be praised; so shall she be saved from her enemies.

PSALM 18:2–3

I pray that You, LORD, are my grandchild's light and her salvation. Whom shall she fear?

PSALM 27:1

--- ❋ ---

I pray, God, that You will strengthen my grandchild according to Your word.

PSALM 119:28

--- ❋ ---

I pray that my grandchild can do all things through Christ who strengthens her.

PHILIPPIANS 4:13

--- ❋ ---

I pray that You, God, will grant my grandchild, according to the riches of Your glory, to be strengthened with might through Your Spirit.

EPHESIANS 3:16

43

TEMPTED

Jesus, You know how to deliver my grandchild out of temptations. I pray right now that You will now and forevermore deliver the grandchild that I love so much from any temptation that he may encounter. I pray Your words for him in this area, and I trust You to do as Your words promise. In Your name I pray. Amen.

**God, in accordance
with Your word . . .**

I pray that You, Lord, know how to deliver my grandchild out of temptations.

2 PETER 2:9

I pray that sin shall not have dominion over my grandchild, for he is not under law but under grace.

ROMANS 6:14

...d, that Your word my grandchild has ...his heart, that he might not sin against ...ou.

PSALM 119:11

———— ❋ ————

I pray, Lord, that my grandchild will not say when he is tempted, "I am tempted by God"; for You cannot be tempted by evil, nor do You Yourself tempt anyone. For he is tempted when he is drawn away by his own desires and enticed. Then, when desire has conceived, it gives birth to sin; and sin, when it is full-grown, brings forth death. I pray that my grandchild will not be deceived.

JAMES 1:13–16

———— ❋ ————

I pray that if my grandchild confesses and forsakes his sins he will have mercy.

PROVERBS 28:13

———— ❋ ————

I pray that if my grandchild confesses his sins, You

are faithful and just to forgive his sins and to cleanse him from all unrighteousness.

1 JOHN 1:9

I pray that no temptation has overtaken my grand-child except such as is common to man; but You, God, are faithful and will not allow him to be tempted beyond what he is able, but with the temptation You will also make the way of escape, that he may be able to bear it.

1 CORINTHIANS 10:13

I pray that my grandchild does not have a High Priest who cannot sympathize with his weak-nesses, but was in all points tempted as he is, yet without sin. Let him therefore come boldly to the throne of grace, that he may obtain mercy and find grace to help in time of need.

HEBREWS 4:15–16

I pray, Jesus, that You are able to aid my grandchild who is tempted.

HEBREWS 2:18

I pray that my grandchild will be sober and vigilant; because his adversary the devil walks about like a roaring lion, seeking whom he may devour. I pray that he will resist him, steadfast in the faith, knowing that the same sufferings are experienced by his Christian brothers in the world.

1 PETER 5:8–9

I pray that my grandchild will be strong in You, Lord, and in Your might. I pray that he will put on Your whole armor, that he may be able to stand against the wiles of the devil and that above all, he takes the shield of faith with which he will be able to quench all the fiery darts of the wicked one.

EPHESIANS 6:10–11, 16

44
TROUBLES

Lord, Your words say that You will allow no more troubles than my grandchild can bear. Today, even now, I pray Your words to overcome any troubles my grandchild may have. Please honor Your words in my prayers, and take care of her and strengthen her. It is in the authority of the name of Jesus that I pray. Amen.

God, in accordance with Your word . . .

I pray that my grandchild shall obtain joy and gladness and that sorrow and sighing shall flee away.

ISAIAH 51:11

———————— ❀ ————————

I pray that my grandchild will be anxious for nothing, but in everything by prayer and supplication, with thanksgiving, will let her requests be made known to You, God, and Your peace, which surpasses all understanding, will guard her heart and mind through Christ Jesus.

PHILIPPIANS 4:6–7

I pray, God, that You will comfort my grandchild in all her tribulation, that she may be able to comfort those who are in any trouble, with the comfort with which she herself is comforted by You.

2 CORINTHIANS 1:3–4

I pray, God, that my grandchild does not worry about tomorrow, for tomorrow will worry about its own things.

MATTHEW 6:34

I pray that all things work together for good to my grandchild who loves You, God, to she who is called according to Your purpose.

ROMANS 8:28

I pray that my grandchild will be glad and rejoice in Your mercy, for You have considered her trouble. You have known her soul in adversities, and have not shut her up into the hand of the enemy; You have set her feet in a wide place.

PSALM 31:7–8

---- ❀ ----

I pray that my grandchild's help comes from You, LORD, who made heaven and earth.

PSALM 121:2

---- ❀ ----

I pray that my grandchild will come boldly to the throne of grace, that she may obtain mercy and find grace to help in time of need.

HEBREWS 4:16

---- ❀ ----

I pray, God, that my grandchild will cast all her cares upon You, for You care for her.

1 PETER 5:7

45
WAITING ON GOD

Heavenly Father, I really do believe that the most important thing that I can do is to pray Your very words and thoughts over my grandchild. My prayers today will be Your words. Hear my prayers, and help my grandchild to wait on You. I pray everything in Jesus' wonderful name. Amen.

God, in accordance
with Your word . . .

I pray, God, that my grandchild will say in that day: "Behold, this is my God; I have waited for Him, and He will save me. This is the LORD; I have waited for Him. I will be glad and rejoice in His salvation."

ISAIAH 25:9

❋

I pray that my grandchild has become a partaker

of Christ if he holds the beginning of his confidence steadfast to the end.

HEBREWS 3:14

I pray that my grandchild waits for You, LORD, that his soul waits, and in Your word he does hope.

PSALM 130:5

I pray that my grandchild will wait on You, LORD, and that he will be of good courage. I pray also that You will strengthen his heart.

PSALM 27:14

I pray, God, that my grandchild's soul waits silently for You alone and that his expectation is from You.

PSALM 62:5

I pray, O God, that my grandchild will hold fast to the confession of his hope without wavering, for You who promised are faithful.

HEBREWS 10:23

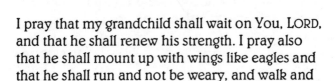

I pray that my grandchild shall wait on You, LORD, and that he shall renew his strength. I pray also that he shall mount up with wings like eagles and that he shall run and not be weary, and walk and not faint.

ISAIAH 40:31

I pray that my grandchild's soul waits for You, LORD, that You are his help and his shield.

PSALM 33:20

46

WORRIED

Most Precious God, I pray Your very words over the worries of my grandchild. You have promised to not let her heart be troubled if she will cast her cares on You. Based on Your words I pray that all worry will flee from her and that her joy will return to her. All of my prayers I pray in Jesus' name. Amen.

**God, in accordance
with Your word . . .**

I pray, God, that my grandchild will not let her heart be troubled.

JOHN 14:1

———————— ❋ ————————

I pray that my grandchild will lie down in peace, and sleep; for You alone, O LORD, make her dwell in safety.

PSALM 4:8

I pray that my grandchild will cast all her cares upon You, God, for You care for her.

1 PETER 5:7

I pray that You, God, will keep my grandchild in perfect peace, she whose mind is stayed on You, because she trusts in You.

ISAIAH 26:3

I pray, God, that my grandchild will let Your peace rule in her heart.

COLOSSIANS 3:15

I pray that my grandchild will be anxious for nothing, but in everything by prayer and supplication, with thanksgiving, let her requests be made known to You, God, and Your peace, which surpasses all understanding, will guard her heart and mind in Christ Jesus.

PHILIPPIANS 4:6–7

I pray, God, that You shall supply all my grand-child's needs according to Your riches in glory by Christ Jesus.

PHILIPPIANS 4:19

I pray that my grandchild will not worry about her life, what she will eat or what she will drink; nor about her body, what she will put on. I pray that she will seek first Your kingdom, God, and Your righteousness, and all these things shall be added to her.

MATTHEW 6:25, 33

I pray, Lord, that when my grandchild lies down, she will not be afraid. I pray that she will lie down and her sleep will be sweet.

PROVERBS 3:24

Seminars conducted by Lee Roberts include "Praying God's Will," "Avoiding Failure in Your Christian Walk," and "The Businessman, the Salesman, and God!"

More information on these seminars can be obtained by writing Lee Roberts, P.O. Box 671465, Marietta, GA 30067-0025, or by calling 404-956-8550.